The Summer Cottage
Retreats of the 1000 Islands

The Summer Cottage
Retreats of the 1000 Islands

KATHLEEN QUIGLEY

PHOTOGRAPHY BY JAMES SCHERZI

RIZZOLI
NEW YORK

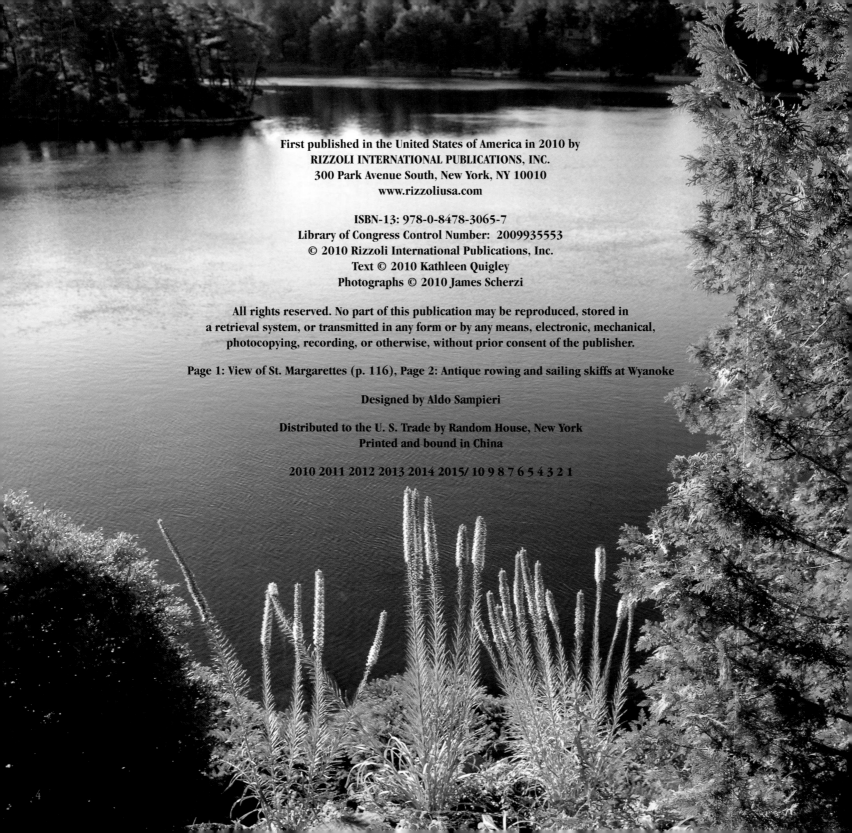

First published in the United States of America in 2010 by
RIZZOLI INTERNATIONAL PUBLICATIONS, INC.
300 Park Avenue South, New York, NY 10010
www.rizzoliusa.com

ISBN-13: 978-0-8478-3065-7
Library of Congress Control Number: 2009935553
© 2010 Rizzoli International Publications, Inc.
Text © 2010 Kathleen Quigley
Photographs © 2010 James Scherzi

Page 1: View of St. Margarettes (p. 116), Page 2: Antique rowing and sailing skiffs at Wyanoke

Designed by Aldo Sampieri

Distributed to the U. S. Trade by Random House, New York
Printed and bound in China

2010 2011 2012 2013 2014 2015/ 10 9 8 7 6 5 4 3 2 1

Contents

Introduction

There is the considerable cachet of island living. "It is your own world," says an owner of a private island in the Thousand Islands. While the cottage at Pine Island is a replica of a 1930s Long Island residence, it rises a dramatic eighty feet above the St. Lawrence River. Breaking away from a large house party, this island dweller strolls the nature trail hewn through granite on the forested fringes of the island. Passing through groves of birch and pine, an eagle takes flight; and a passing ship plies the waters. A stone's throw away, Little Pine Island, with two trees, beckons as a place for rowing excursions. At the boathouse, a fleet of boats is at the ready for river expeditions or trips to the mainland.

In this remote region known as the Thousand Islands, an archipelago of close to one thousand nine hundred islands in the St. Lawrence River straddles the U.S. and Canadian borders in northern New York and Ontario, roughly a fifty-mile stretch. The stunning beauty and quiet majesty of the mighty river and its forested islands have inspired its denizens to dream and ruminate. It was called "Monatoana," or "Garden of the Great Spirit," by the Indians. Later French settlers, led by Jacques Cartier, named it "Les Milles Îles."

Left: *A highly embellished cottage at Thousand Island Park*
Page 9: *Belora, built by Nathan Straus, a co-owner of Macy's department store*

The resort era took off in 1872 when George Pullman, the railroad car magnate, invited President Ulysses S. Grant to visit rustic Camp Charming during a reelection year, prompting attention in the press. In the Gilded Age that followed, captains of industry were inspired to create castles and compounds that reflected the exuberance of new fortunes; they arrived by private railroad car and were taken by steam yacht to their islands. In that era, grand hotels flourished, and the *New York Times* reflected on the social whirl and a gilded guest list that enjoyed balls and teas, yacht racing and water carnivals, polo and croquet. A travel guide of the era touted this islandscape with its labyrinth of river passages as "the Venice of America."

"I have traveled the world, and never found anything like it," wrote Charles Goodwin Emery in 1901. A New York tobacco baron, Emery developed Calumet Island with castle and ballroom, as well as the grand Frontenac Hotel on Round Island. At the hotel, guests were offered a telegraph office with direct access to stockbrokers in New York City, and fresh roses were supplied from Emery's greenhouses on Picton Island. The Frontenac fell to fire in 1911, a harbinger of the end of the grand hotel era; and the castle at Calumet disappeared with the tides of time.

However, there remains a fantastical array of resort architecture on the river, often replete with towers and turrets. There is a serendipitous spirit of summer here. A breezy, wide porch decorated with wicker is the primary place for enjoying the pleasures of the season. The cottage is generally sited high on the crest of the island, with former dependencies such as icehouses and caretaker's cottages shielded from the public view as one arrives by boat. Hospitality is legion, privacy is prized, and drop-ins from the mainland are infrequent. Squadrons of staff have been replaced by a loyal few, and the former staff quarters are now additional guest space.

Cleveland Amory, when introducing the Thousand Islands in his book *The Last Resorts*, noted, "small islands, particularly those difficult to reach, have always played a large role in the fulfillment of Newton's Law of Resort Reaction, or the search for social simplicity."

Many of the grand Gilded Age cottages retain a formal front entrance on the river, once the arrival point for large steam yachts that transported the owners. Today the boathouse is often the favored point of entry. Inside, there are show boats, rich with the patina of burnished mahogany; work boats of utilitarian Fiberglass; and antique skiffs for rowing the river. Captains of industry, or their scions, still ply the waters. Cherished cottages are passed down through generations or purchased by those taken at first sight while cruising the river. The lifestyle is relaxed, with cruising the river a popular form of recreation. It is a world where the sound of an engine resonates with a certain cadence—a sign of ownership—and where sounds, silhouettes of islands, and a chart still pave the path along the river. There is a camaraderie among the islanders. "People have love of the river in common," says an owner from Bluff Island.

Environmental groups, such as the Thousand Islands Land Trust (TILT) and Save the River, are helping to conserve a rare way of life and pristine ecosystem. TILT, which owns or holds conservation easements on over seven thousand acres, is opposed to building on islands under one acre. They also own forty-four shoals. Save the River is ever vigilant against winter navigation, as the opening of shipping lanes would threaten fragile shoreline structures.

Nowhere is the restoration ethic more concentrated than at Thousand Island Park, a private resort enclave on Wellesley Island that was added to the National Register of Historic Places in 1982. A variety of cottages—in the Gothic, Eastlake, Queen Anne, and Neoclassical styles—line narrow streets with names like Paradise and Rainbow and are highly ornamented. Exterior alterations are subject to the Preservation/Architectural Review Board. A public pavilion at the water's edge, built in 1875 as a landing for steamships, was restored in recent years. And lately, the restoration of a Carpenter Gothic cottage sparked much interest.

All in all, there appears to be a contemporary renaissance on the river—the beginning of a second golden era. For, as the cadence of the river unfolds, a private paradise awaits.

Left: *The contemporary boathouse at Birkinshaw (p. 64)*

Above: *A recently restored Carpenter Gothic cottage at Thousand Island Park*

Occident, 1874

A sliver of a moon and a wisp of a star are stenciled on the shutters of house on Occident Island, one of the oldest cottages on the river. Here, the sense of a timeless spirit of summer prevails. Old leather-bound logbooks, stamped in gold with the name "Occident," chronicle both the changing seasons on the island and the changing seasons of life, spanning six generations. It is a short boat jaunt from the mainland, yet this venerable cottage—shaded by old oaks and pitch pine trees—is a world removed.

The island saga starts in 1874, when the house was built as a fishing lodge and club, whose list of members comprise the names in front of one logbook. It was utilized as a clubhouse until 1879, when it closed until 1900. It was purchased then by William D. Wilson Sr., an iron worker from Watertown, New York, and great-great-grandfather of current owner of the island. During Wilson's lifetime, he owned five islands on the river, including nearby Orient, and enjoyed exploring the river with a 20' rowboat with canopied top, as well as with the steam yacht *Occident*.

Little has changed. The cottage is oriented toward the fresh south-by-southwest winds off the river, which breeze through on a halcyon summer day as memories flow, over a perusal of the logbooks. The three-sided porch was the focal point for growing up, surrounded by an extended family. Seasons come and go. In October 1903, it is recorded that the island dwellers "shut up 'camp'." In May 1904, the cottage is "opened." Generations, signing their names, gathered for traditional Sunday dinners of chicken and dumplings, and fresh peach ice cream. "The more we are together, the merrier we will be," noted one writer in a logbook in 1927.

While the old water pump has been replaced by hot and cold running water, and a backup electric stove supports the wood stove, the third in a series, there are limited concessions to contemporary living. "We live in a throwaway society," says the island denizen, sitting in the main living/dining room with walls and floors of darkened, wide-board pine. "Here we fix everything." And indeed, a century-old rowing skiff recently has been restored, with the owner's initials painted on the paddles. It floats next to the board and batten boathouse, which has additional bedrooms to supplement those of the cottage.

There is an aura of self-reliance that is intrinsic to island living, a commitment to come and go, regardless of the weather, inclement and fogbound as it may be. When a sudden wind shear, a microburst, struck and left the river powerless, it was back to kerosene lamps, the wood stove, and blocks of ice in the refrigerator at Occident Island—signaling a return to tradition.

Left: *Six generations of family have gathered on this porch to enjoy the simple pleasures of summer.*

Page 16: *The Occident logbook chronicles the changing seasons on the island. The first entry in the log dates back to 1874.*

Page 17: *The iron wood-burning stove is a vestige from another era.*

Left: *From an old iron bed to vintage clothing, "everything is here that was here," says an owner.*

Right: *The Orange Room has exposed pine beams and contains a collection of old books and memorabilia.*

Page 20: *The Occident boathouse has additional family living space and houses a century-old skiff.*

Page 21: *The Rock Island lighthouse stands sentry on the horizon.*

Centennial, 1876

Centennial, built in 1876, celebrates America's one hundredth anniversary, and its exterior and interiors are inspired by the exuberance of a young nation. It is sited on a narrow street in Thousand Island Park, where the village green slopes down to the river. A private resort enclave on 145 acres on Wellesley Island, it grew from a Methodist campsite of tents. Today it is noted as a colony of some 320 buildings, highly individualized with decorative embellishment, and listed on the National Register of Historic Places. Centennial dates to the park's earliest era. In the same family since the 1890s, it had fallen on hard times when acquired by the current owners in 1998; the previous owner then was willing to part with the cottage for back taxes.

The previous owner explained that old photographs depicted the cottage as painted red, white, and blue, which was a starting point for the current owners, who never could find the documentation. A painter discovered that the battens had been blue, however. Inside, all the tongue and groove pine woodwork, from floors and walls to ceilings, is original. The living room and upstairs interiors have never been painted. A tin ceiling was added to the living room, in keeping with the decoration of that era. Outside, the sunburst decoration is original to the cottage, and its color was revealed as yellow under existing paint. A new five-point star was added to the cottage skirt for whimsy. It is believed that the enclosed porch is a relatively new addition; the first porch would have been open to the elements.

Two fires in the 1910s claimed many buildings in the neighboring park and, while Centennial was spared, it was discovered that the roof had sustained numerous burn marks. A round wooden table on the front porch was found to have extensive fire damage when stripped, and thought to be from one of the two grand hotels that once dominated the park.

The dining area, in keeping with the character of the cottage, has a patriotic theme of red, white, and blue, exemplified by the American flag.

The master bedroom opens onto a sleeping porch, decorated in a sunburst motif.

In the early years of the cottage, the porch would have been open to the elements.

Little Lehigh, 1879

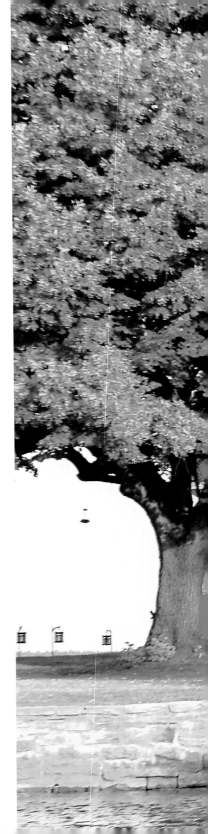

With a fortune derived from the Lehigh Railroad, Asa Packer, the founder of Lehigh University, purchased three islands in the St. Lawrence for use as a family compound. Little Lehigh, at almost one acre, is connected to Sport Island by an iron suspension bridge. Like Sport Island, nearby Idlewild Island was larger and became known for its grass tennis courts.

In keeping with the vagaries of fashion, Little Lehigh was changed from Stick Style to Queen Anne in the 1890s when owned by Packer's daughter, Mary Packer Cummings. It functioned largely as an adjunct to Sport Island, and it is conceivable that Mrs. Cummings would have walked over for dinner each evening. In another era, the owner believes the cottage functioned as a gentlemen's retreat. "It was a retreat for the men, where they could play cards, and a getaway where they could plan their next hunting or fishing trip," says the owner.

With little setback from the river, there is the constant murmur of the lap of water upon the shore. "It is so tranquil," says the owner. In the living room, a Victorian settee is a vestige of the past, with arms that fold down so it can be used as a cot. To the rear, a new kitchen with a wall of curving glass windows was added in the 1970s, enclosing a porch. Upstairs, three bedrooms are ensconced high above the water, with balconies overlooking the river. "You feel like you are on a ship, high above the water," says the owner.

Projects are rife and include restoring a 34' antique Chris Craft, the *Lehigh*. The 1879 cottage has benefited from foundation revitalization, insulation, soundproofing, and seawall rebuilding. "You utilize and maintain and repair," says the owner of the saga of island life. For the wife—whose parents reside on neighboring Grenadier Island and who grew up touring the islands—Little Lehigh always exuded a special cachet. Buying it was "a dream come true."

The scrolled design of the front door is reiterated on balcony doors of the cottage, which originally was part of a family compound on three islands.

Left: *The new kitchen with a wall of curving glass windows was added in the 1970s, enclosing a porch.*

Page 48: *The White Room opens onto a balcony high above the river and, according to an owner, gives the feeling of living on a ship.*

Page 49: *A guest bedroom is paneled in traditional beadboard.*

Left: *River breezes and the sound of water lapping against the banks add a sense of calm to the dining alcove on the wraparound porch.*

Right: *Classical columns line the front porch, which overlooks Sport Island.*

Hasbrouck Cottage, Manhattan Island, 1870s

Manhattan was the first island in the region cultivated for recreation—it was bought in 1855 by Seth Green, a prominent fish culturist. He constructed a cottage, still extant, and then sold the island to J. I. Hasbrouck of Ogdensburg, New York, and Judge J. C. Spencer of New York City. The latter built a cottage in 1870; the date of Hasbrouck Cottage is hence hypothesized to the 1870s.

The picturesque cottage has a two-tiered porch with balconies that hang above the water and face west for sunsets. Framed by mature trees, the cottage is set on a slightly undulating landscape. "It has a simple, romantic, easy spirit to it," says the owner. "The builder thought out the details in the railings, staircases, and side windows." A primary decorative detail of the board and batten cottage is the abundant spindlework, or gingerbread.

It is believed that the builder also culled inspiration from pattern books, melding styles. While the late Queen Anne transitional cottage has a symmetrical waterside facade, the entrance by land has the look of a bungalow. The boathouse reflects a later era.

In 1958 the six-acre Manhattan Island was purchased by Robert Peach, a regional airline owner and executive. While some island holdings have been sold, including the Hasbrouck cottage, today the original Seth Green cottage is home to a family member.

An antique wicker swing, fanned by river breezes, is located on the front porch.

*Left: A bedroom door
with a brass knob is
draped in antique lace.*

*Right: There are four
bedrooms in the cottage.*

The board and batten cottage is faceted with detail, from its side staircase to finials.

The detailing of the balusters is reflected on the porch at sunset.

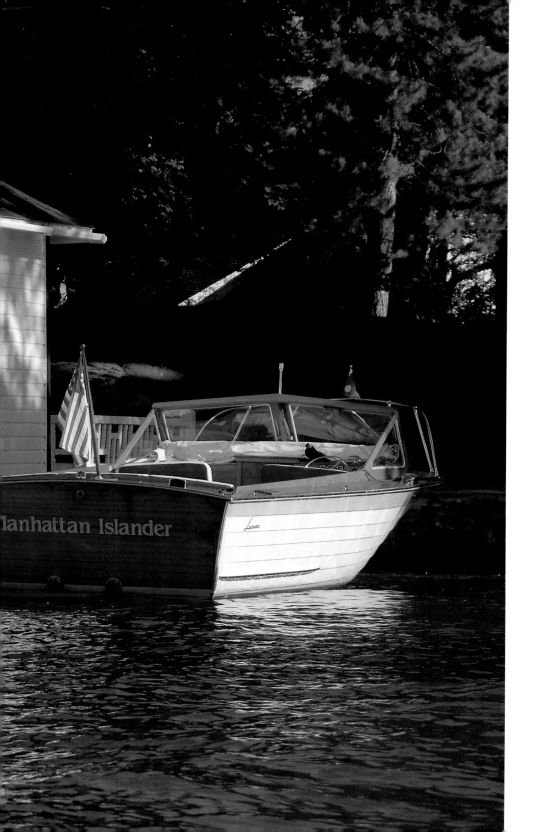

The boathouse with dormer windows is of a later era than the cottage.

Birkinshaw, 1880

The island complex is named Birkinshaw—an Indian word for a grove of silver birch trees, which grow on the craggy site and line the river. The name is painted on a rock in front of the cottage, sited on multiple building lots in Westminster Park for a 270' panorama of the river. "The house was built on one large boulder; it hasn't moved for 125 years," says the owner. The community of Westminster Park was bought in 1874 by a Presbyterian stock company. In 1879, as a building boom began, the land was deeded to G. D. Higgins of Rome, New York.

The tiny, historic boathouse with barrel-vaulted roof, originally the skiff house, was built in 1880 and is among the early structures of Westminster Park, where residents originally came and tented. A century later, in 1982, the boathouse was sitting in the river and bereft of docks when current owners responded to an advertisement for a "small Victorian estate, suitable for a hunting or fishing lodge." Antiquated and eclectic, the main structure and boathouse were restored; new decorative details included tin ceilings and scrolled porch brackets.

The owners then purchased an antique wooden boat with a surprise provenance. As registry papers were proffered, they became reacquainted with a family boating legacy. When the identity of the former owner—the grandfather of the current owner—was revealed, she bought it instantly. Now restored, *Black & Tan*, a 1951 Hubert Johnson utility, takes it name from its colors—black sides and a tan canopy. Today the boat is rife with "lots of memories," according to the owner, and enjoyed by grandchildren.

Because the tiny, historic boathouse was too narrow for *Black & Tan*, a new boathouse was designed by Grater Architects of Clayton, New York, to emulate the architecture of the cottage and former boathouse. "It was a match of everything, including the gingerbread," said the owner. The new boathouse, with a large recreation room atop the boat slip, has the same steeply pitched roof with finials and gable decoration, as well as the same sawn porch balustrades that rim the cottage.

The boathouse abuts deep "good water," with a depth of thirty to forty feet. On the perimeter of the property is a tiny 150' canal passage, an island shortcut for rowing skiffs.

The contemporary boathouse, seen here, has the same building details as the historic, cedar board and batten cottage, from balusters to gable decoration.

A later addition, the porch has scrolled
brackets, balusters, and mahogany flooring
that echo design elements of the historic
cottage. The coffee table is the former engine
cover for the owner's boat, Black & Tan.

Left page:

Top: *The contemporary boathouse features a recreation room with fir wainscoting and cedar trim.*

Bottom: *Tin ceilings made from antique presses were added to the living room.*

This page: *The back porch is original to the cottage, and is shaded by woods.*

Page 72: *The barrel-vaulted skiff house is among the earliest structures in Westminster Park.*

Sally's Surprise, 1886

An antique fish, emblazoned with the name "Sally's Surprise," hangs over the piazza of this 1886 cottage in Thousand Island Park. Over a century after its construction, it was renovated and refurbished by the new owner, so much so that when his wife arrived, the cottage was in move-in condition—hence the name "Sally's Surprise." The cottage has functioned both as a private residence and as a small hotel encompassing several neighboring cottages along the river.

While the private resort community has many diminutive cottages with fanciful fretwork, this residence appealed to the owners with its larger river lot and architecture that reflected the vocabulary of the developing park, including a tower—a popular feature. The piazza, which differs from a porch by being low to the ground and having no railing or enclosure, was an evolution of the early, tented platforms in the park. The community began as a campsite in a salubrious setting on Wellesley Island and was followed by the building of cottages from the 1870s though 1920.

The cottage was first owned by the Edwin Holden family, patrons of the park who were also the benefactors and builders of the chapel and the library. Their yacht, *Lotus Seeker*, was reportedly the fastest boat on the St. Lawrence in 1898. In 1915 the cottage became part of the Rochester Hotel and operated as such until the 1960s, at which time it became a private residence once again. By 1999, when purchased by the current owners, it was in a serious state of disrepair.

Along with extensive renovations—including a new foundation, piazza, and fireplace—attention was given to reconfiguring the rooms of the former hotel to meet the needs of a private residence. An interior wall was removed to create a large open space in the main living area, which has bird's eye maple floors and two original pianos. Upstairs, fourteen bedrooms were redesigned to create eight contemporary bedrooms, one of which is called "the dormitory." On the third floor, slanted 11' ceilings create a sculptural effect, and a trap door leads to the tower above a bedroom. One bedroom has a small stage. Throughout the cottage, there is tongue and groove paneling, and sash windows of wavy antique glass are open to balmy breezes off the St. Lawrence River.

Left: *The dining room table, found in an antiques shop, was added during the cottage's complete refurbishment.*
Page 78: *A wall was removed to create an open space, reconfiguring a former small hotel into a private residence.*

*A bedroom, with slanting eaves,
has a small stage.*

Pullman Island, 1888

It began as a quest for a fishing spot on the river, yet turned into a great discovery as the overgrown estate of George Pullman on Pullman Island came into view. The railroad car magnate, known for his Pullman Palace Car Company, had put the Thousand Islands on the resort map in 1872 when he invited President Ulysses S. Grant to visit rustic Camp Charming. Subsequently, in 1888, he built the six-story Castle Rest, with a tower that dominated three acres, verdant with trees he had planted. Remaining now for the boatmen was the commodious building that had served as the staff quarters, with kitchen, a skiff house, a recreation building with billiards room, and a stone gazebo at the water's edge. It took eight years of expressed interest to secure the sale of the island in 1972 from the Pullman estate heirs.

Today Pullman Island is enjoying a renaissance, brought about by a family now ensconced there for thirty-eight years, who enjoy the same scenic views of the river from the terrace that Pullman had shared with President Grant. "It gets into your soul, and you can't shake it," says a son of the owner, who treasures his summers there.

In August 1888, Pullman dedicated the island structures to his mother. That year a newspaper, the *Watertown Herald*, in referring to the house then in construction, suggested that an onlooker would think it an " English shooting lodge." After the death of Pullman in 1897, his oldest daughter, Florence, inherited the property; she enjoyed it with her husband, Frank Lowden, an attorney who was elected governor of Illinois. In 1906 Lowden commissioned a 38' Hutchinson launch known as *Monitor*, which is now a Castle Rest legacy.

By the mid 1950s, Pullman descendants were ready to part with the castle. It was dynamited. Also razed was the original Pullman boathouse, a replica of a railroad sleeping car. Today the castle's original rubble foundation provides the parameters for the terraces and gardens; the outdoor spaces follow the blueprint of the house. Down by the river and stone gazebo is the formal steam yacht landing, with sweeping path up the island that would take guests to the castle. Replacing the original tower is a new three-story tower with similarly staggered and wavy shingles on the exterior; inside is a sitting room, library, and bedroom.

The main house today, the former staff quarters, is accessed by a small spiral staircase that leads to a hallway lined with commodious bedrooms and a bathroom. These rooms progress onto a riverside porch before exiting down another tiny staircase. The Round Room is named for its shape.

The recreation building, formerly the billiards room, has a ceiling that was painted with vines by a French artist commissioned by Pullman; the artwork has been conserved. Today the room is used for dormitory-style sleeping quarters. A skiff house, replete with old fire hoses that are still operable, has been adapted with a second-story addition that features an A-frame sitting room dominated by an historic, award-winning canoe that came with the property.

The original paths meander the island, where Pullman had directed the planting of trees—pines, maples, and oaks. He dedicated them to family members, noted on brass medallions affixed to the trees. Today a sense of living history prevails on the island, with recent excitement at finding one of the medallions as the grounds were being raked. And the new tower evokes the architecture and spirit of the former tower that once loomed high above the river, a beacon of the early resort.

Page 24: *A focal point of the island compound is a contemporary tower; it evokes the spirit of the former tower that loomed above Castle Rest, Pullman's cottage that was razed in the mid-1950s.*

This page: *The new tower has a sitting room, library, and bedroom—all paneled in red fir with wainscoting.*

Page 28: *In the former staff cottage, which now houses the kitchen and bedrooms, a spiral staircase leads to a hallway lined with bedrooms, including the Round Room (not shown) named for its shape.*

Page 29: *In the former billiards room, which now serves as a dormitory for guests, a ceiling painting that Pullman commissioned has been restored.*

This page: *The contemporary A-frame sitting room is an addition atop the skiff house; the canoe, ordered for the island, is from the 1930s.*

Opposite: *A new dock can accommodate* Monitor, *a 1906 38' Hutchinson launch that is a Pullman family legacy.*

Left: *The former staff cottage was built of stone from island quarries; the wavy shingles have a staggered pattern, which was replicated on the contemporary tower.*

Right: *The terrace overlooks the wooded island, with trees planted by Pullman and dedicated to his family members.*

Rivercroft,
Round Island, 1888

R ivercroft has a commanding presence at the head of Round Island. With a name derived from the Scottish word for a small farm, it was part of a triumvirate of cottages known as "The Three Sisters" that included the Dutch-inspired Brunarche and Pinecroft, the latter destroyed by fire in the 1970s.

The Shingle Style cottage was built in 1888. Early owner Jacob Hays was also an owner of the grand Frontenac Hotel (also on Round Island), which he acquired at a mortgage foreclosure sale. When Hays sold the cottage in 1900, the *New York Times* described it as "one of the handsomest on the St. Lawrence River." A subsequent Rivercroft owner, James B. Edge, was a vice president and director at DuPont; the island remained in his family from 1928 to 1971, during which time Pinecroft was also owned by the same clan. Each summer the family convened there for the last two weeks in August. "It was more of an edict than an invitation," says grandson Edwin Ladley, who fondly recalls fishing trips with their boatman, Joe Robbins.

The current owners were looking for a place to tie up a boat and tent, when they came across Rivercroft some thirty years ago. The cottage beckoned with secret passageways and an upstairs balcony trimmed with rope, but then it was boarded up on a wilderness of five acres. Today it is a place for all seasons: the owners are likely to be on the river even as the snow is falling, and have named the former caretaker's cottage Wintercroft, now a haven in the off-season.

The cottage has a striking feature of Shingle Style architecture, the living hall, which is dominated by a freestanding Imperial staircase with lathe-turned spindles; it leads up to a stained-glass window at the landing. Downstairs, the entrance hall has a fireplace with egg and dart molding. Beadboard interiors radiate with the warmth of wood. Off the living hall is the dining room, notable for it blue and white Delft tile fireplace, bow window, and darkened oak walls. Blue glassware atop the fireplace is among the collectibles, which also include a leather chaise longue from the Frontenac Hotel, which fell to fire in 1911.

Reiterating the construction of the cottage, the skiff house has hand-cut shingles. Antique wavy glass in the eyebrow windows looks in on fishing poles and old fishing lures swept in from the river onto rocky shores—"a gift from the sea," says the owner.

In the entrance or living hall, a freestanding Imperial staircase leads up to a stained-glass window.

The dining room has darkened oak walls
and a Delft tile fireplace.

Pages 88-89: The skiff house has wavy hand-
cut shingles, and curving eyebrow windows.

Bosun
On Guard

Neh Mahbin, Comfort Island, 1890

L ong lauded as a beauty of the river, Neh Mahbin has two grand entrances—the first formal entrance on the American Narrows was designed for steam yachts; the second entrance, the boathouse, has evolved. "The boathouse is now the threshold of the property, and of the entire island," says the owner of Neh Mahbin, who purchased the island at auction sixteen years ago after it had fallen into disrepair. Initially interested in the boathouse, he and his family have created a compound that is a showcase on the river and designed for entertaining. The reconstructed water tower houses a sound system that transmits music to speakers mounted in the trees and gardens. The cottage faces west for stunning sunsets. Special spaces framed by flowers abound as one walks the grounds. Beyond tunnels planted with wisteria and roses, there is a view of Boldt Castle in the distance.

The first Neh Mahbin fell to fire in 1890. Its owner, James Oliphant, a well-known New York stockbroker, rebuilt the house in the Neoclassical style, with monumental pilasters on each corner. Meanwhile, the Shingle Style boathouse retains vestiges of the character of the original house. Inside the boathouse is a wooden skiff marked with the name "J Oliphant." From the boathouse, great urns of flowers flank the sweeping stone steps that lead up to the cottage. The urns were collected from around the world—from Paris, France to Bouckville, New York. The cottage is sited high on the island. "It's like being on the bridge of a big yacht," says the owner.

Inside, the living room is a near-circle and framed by Ionic columns; another feature of the room is the plasterwork frieze. A vintage blue paint was chosen for the woodwork, echoed softly in the sofas' color. The seagrass carpet was brought by barge, requiring a large crew. Both ceiling and plasterwork have been restored. The adjacent dining room, with 1907 Tiffany wallpaper, has been kept as original as possible. In the kitchen, a new tin ceiling was added. Outside, columns were added to expand a porch for outdoor dining. Upstairs, some of the eleven bedrooms have two doors: one is louvered to allow the river breezes to waft through the rooms.

The crew quarters of the boathouse are now used as guest quarters, with the former kitchen and dining room made into additional bedrooms. A balcony overhangs the river. The boathouse has new eyebrow windows, dormers, and a slate roof. It also has been reinforced with steel. And indeed, while each season heralds in a new project, a special impetus the summer of 2007 was preparing the cottage for the owner's birthday party—a weekend event for 275 guests entitled "A Midsummer's Night Dream," culminating in fireworks and dancing at Boldt Castle. "We had tables set out on the lawn and gardens, lit with hundreds of candles . . . it was just magical." The current owner enjoys mixing friends from around the world with the islanders. "There is a history of hospitality on the river," he says.

Antique urns filled with petunias flank a sweep of stone staircase leading from the boathouse to the cottage.

A parade of rocking chairs overlooks the Thousand Islands Bridge, connecting the United States and Canada.

Left page:

Top: *The near-circular living room has curving glass windows, a rounded fireplace, and a plasterwork ceiling that has been restored.*

Bottom: *Each end of the interior porch opens onto gardens.*

This page:

Right: *The dining room has original Louis Comfort Tiffany wallpaper.*

Page 98: *The owner has amassed a collection of antique boats, from rowing skiffs and canoes to long-deck launches.*

Casa Blanca, 1892

A grand Gilded Age cottage on Cherry Island, Casa Blanca bears the imprint of Louis Marx. An American tobacco and sugar planter in Cuba, Marx maintained a residence in New York City along with his river cottage. With a sense of the theatrical, he installed an electric fountain on the front lawn, which had been exhibited at the World's Fair in Chicago. The event was noted in *The New York Times*, as well as by onlookers who enjoyed a slow parade along the river from their steam yachts.

Over half a century later, Casa Blanca was viewed as a white elephant and, in 1962, was purchased by the current owners to avert its potential razing. Indeed, it was purchased without any sight of the magnificent river views, as a cantankerous caretaker refused to raise the blinds of the wide wraparound porch. Today that expansive porch with sky blue ceiling is a focal point of island living, from entertaining to ship and sunset watching. There are tiny, old wicker chairs set out for six grandchildren. Nearby, hammocks are strung along the path to the old stone gazebo. "The beauty of the river . . . you never get over it," says the owner. Of the porch, she added, "we spend as much time as we can here." Casa Blanca can accommodate some thirty-five house guests. And, broad lawns lend themselves to croquet.

Inside, vestiges of the Gilded Age remain. "Nothing is changed," says the owner. The outdoor terrace opens onto the reception hall, with ceilings and side walls of pressed tin. With music the major mode of entertainment since its building, there are two player pianos in the reception hall. A pump organ graces the dining room, a space notable for its bentwood Thonet furniture from Vienna and Fostoria glass, which frequently adorns the table. A collection of blue and white Meissen china is stored in the butler's pantry. Nearby is the butler's pull station, once the control center of the cottage when a retinue of servants lived in or arrived from town by day.

The reception hall is flanked by the library and the billiards room, formerly the music room. At the rear of the hall, the paneled staircase has a stained-glass window at the landing, with a scene depicting pheasants on the river in the early morning light. Upstairs, a labyrinth of master suites and bedrooms with marble sinks unfolds. There is a screened sleeping porch that draws in salubrious summer breezes.

Today a small staff is diligent about maintaining Casa Blanca, whether polishing the silver or servicing the fleet of boats. Located across the island, the boathouse, with crew quarters, is home to *America*, a 55' Blue Water, and *Lady Edith*, a 1946 Hutchinson—both used for runs up and down the river. As a doyenne of the river sits on her terrace, she reminisces about fabled island neighbors on the horizon—a stretch of river known as "Millionaire's Row."

This gargoyle is part of the elaborate stonework at the river's edge.

Left: *The ceiling of the porch traditionally has been painted a sky blue.*

Right: *With music historically being the mode of entertainment at Casa Blanca, the reception hall has two player pianos.*

Left: *An old brass bed is among a treasure trove of antiques.*

Right: *"Nothing is changed," says the owner, of a timeless vignette featuring the portrait of a former owner's granddaughter.*

A sleeping porch on the water encapsulates the essence of summer.

A second-story porch is open to the gentle breezes off the river. Inside the cedar-shingled yacht house, a sitting area overlooks the yacht slip. Furnished with old wicker, it is a place for gatherings, including impromptu music sessions. The former crew quarters also include four bedrooms, one of which fronts the river. A fifth bedroom was removed, in keeping with the original structure. With the constant lap of water in the yacht slip, the orientation to the river has been retained both inside and out.

The living addition downstairs has beadboard walls and is dominated by a great 1930s fireplace of Potsdam, New York, stone, now decorated with old freshwater ship lanterns collected by the owner. Up some steps is a small galley kitchen.

The boathouse rocks gently on its timber crib, which is filled with stones. It has been rebuilt twice, most recently with the help of Escape Marine. To rebuild it, interlocking steel pilings were brought in to stabilize the crib structure. And while the yacht house originally housed the steam yacht *Wyanoke I*, today it is home to *Wyanoke*, a 1956 Hutchinson 26' utility.

On the compound is a skiff house with eyebrow window. True to its original function, it protects eight wooden St. Lawrence skiffs from the elements. Included are two sailing skiffs. While collectibles today, they also are avidly enjoyed on the river by the current owner. Nearby is the stone pump house, once used for pumping water to a cistern atop the island.

The rare, surviving steam yacht house has a second-story porch, overlooking a quiet stretch of river.

The yacht house is set on a timber crib filled with stones. The small skiff house shelters a collection of antique rowing and sailing skiffs, avidly enjoyed by the owner on the river today.

St. Margarettes, 1896

S pare and sculptural, this cottage with Norman influences was built in 1896 and has been likened to a little stone castle. It was built on a great rock promontory with a facade of native granite. Inscribed in the foundation is a cornerstone with the letter T, a reference to the name of the builder, William H. Taylor, a doctor from northern New York. A tower, with painted brick quoining and lintels and an oculus window, houses the living room and master bedroom.

As the days unfold, activity flows between two porches. The breakfast porch is oriented for smaller gatherings and for the sunrise. At the other end, the western porch is oriented for sunsets and big family dinners. This larger porch also serves as an open-air living room.

Inside, the living room in the tower is focused on the fireplace, a meeting place when it is time to batten down the hatches. All the beaded paneling is vertical and curving, making conversation and acoustics easy. Whereas, in the billiards room, the paneling is horizontal.

A contemporary boathouse, designed by Grater Architects, was inspired by a Norman keep and houses an artist's studio above. "There's an incredible sense of well-being when you get into your boathouse at night, particularly in adverse conditions," said the architect, son of the owners, in an interview with *The New York Times*. A fleet of boats transports the family between St. Margarettes and rustic Halfway Island nearby, which they also own in quiet Chippewa Bay.

The tower, which houses the living room and master bedroom,
has an oculus window and painted brick quoins.

In the living room of the tower, the beaded paneling is vertical and curving.

Left: *The billiards room
has horizontal paneling.*

Right: *French doors open
onto the screened
western porch, which is
used for family dinners.*

The recently added boathouse was inspired by a Norman keep, and houses an artist's studio.

Left: *With a penchant for the color green, a former owner stained this bathroom vanity.*

Right: *The bay window of a bedroom overlooks the children's play area and a dollhouse that was created from the former fishing guide's cottage.*

Always, 1898

The cottage was built in 1898 and had a succession of owners until purchased in 1926 by Max Winslow, a Los Angeles music publisher. That August when Winslow invited a beleaguered honeymooner, his colleague Irving Berlin, to visit, it was featured on the front page of the *Los Angeles Times*. Berlin had attracted sensational media attention when honeymooning in Europe following his marriage to heiress Ellin Mackay. Weathering her father's objections to marriage to a songwriter, he wrote the love song "Always" for her and assigned her the royalties.

Many of Berlin's songs were composed in the Thousand Islands. For years he had been a visitor to a small hotel in Ivy Lea on the Canadian side, noted *The New York Times* when it announced the impending visit to the St. Lawrence Park cottage. "It is a bungalow, within a stone's throw of the St. Lawrence River; with ten rooms, and is set among tall pines," noted the newspaper. "It is painted a dark green, with white trimming, and looks like a charming little 'love nest.'"

While the music room has since been dismantled, the cottage continues to exude a sense of serene simplicity, augmented by the word "Always" inscribed on a plaque on the front facade. An Irish flag and a U.S. flag fly side by side. In deference to Berlin's visit, an MGM mascot dog sits on the front lawn next to an antique phonograph. Elsewhere on the property, the former fishing guide's cottage has been adapted as a dollhouse and children's playhouse.

Today four generations of a family enjoy the simple days of summer, with games like playing ship trivia from the wraparound porch of the cottage, as passing freighters ply the waters. The five-bedroom cottage has traditional pine beadboard interiors. There is an old, black rotary telephone, and for years there was no television. "It is family-oriented, a place to converge and have closeness," says a daughter of the owner. "It's the reason that we are here."

Left: *A rotary telephone, a vestige of an earlier era, sits atop a Stickley desk.*

Page 130: *"It is a glorious place to have dinner as the sun comes across the water and is reflected in the French doors," says the owner, of the dining room with oak table and rush-bottom ladder-back chairs.*

Page 131: *Family members test their ship trivia from the wraparound porch, as passing freighters ply the international waterway.*

Left: *With a penchant for the color green, a former owner stained this bathroom vanity.*

Right: *The bay window of a bedroom overlooks the children's play area and a dollhouse that was created from the former fishing guide's cottage.*

Sunnyside, 1902

Sunnyside was designed in high-style Shingle Style by architect Henry Hardenbergh, whose commissions included The Plaza Hotel, The Dakota apartment building, and the Waldorf-Astoria (all in New York City). It was built for a Cleveland, Ohio, steel maker, Samuel Brown, whose wife kept a detailed diary of life on the island, then known as Hadassah. A guest book from those days reveals a steady stream of visitors from New York City and Cleveland, with one 1903 guest writing, "May each year increase your happiness and the joy of your island home."

Sunnyside was originally surrounded by an open porch, now partially enclosed. Shallow bay windows give a wavy effect to the exterior. Inside, the living room has a massive stone fireplace; the building material is believed to be from George Boldt's quarry on Oak Island. A bookcase is built into it and filled with old books. The living room Stickley furniture is a later reissue of the original design. In the dining room is the original 1910 Gustav Stickley dining set, with china cabinet filled with china from Hong Kong and China. The butler's pantry originally led to a kitchen with wood stove and servant's quarters beyond, which are now winterized for year-round enjoyment of the island.

Upstairs, a sitting area features an original Stickley desk, and overlooks the St. Lawrence River. The bedrooms, each with a marble sink, have bay windows overlooking the water.

Sunnyside is set on the rugged crest of a two-and-a-half-acre island. Outbuildings include a stone caretaker's cottage, an icehouse where cut ice was once stored, and a boathouse, home to a 1991 reproduction Hacker Craft, *Sundown*. More landscaping—an apple tree and a flowering dogwood—is being added to the eclectic mix of trees on the island, which include mountain ash, maple, oak, and pine. The view is of both U.S. and Canadian channels. "We have the best of both worlds," says the owner.

The curving porch overlooks both the American and Canadian channels of the river.

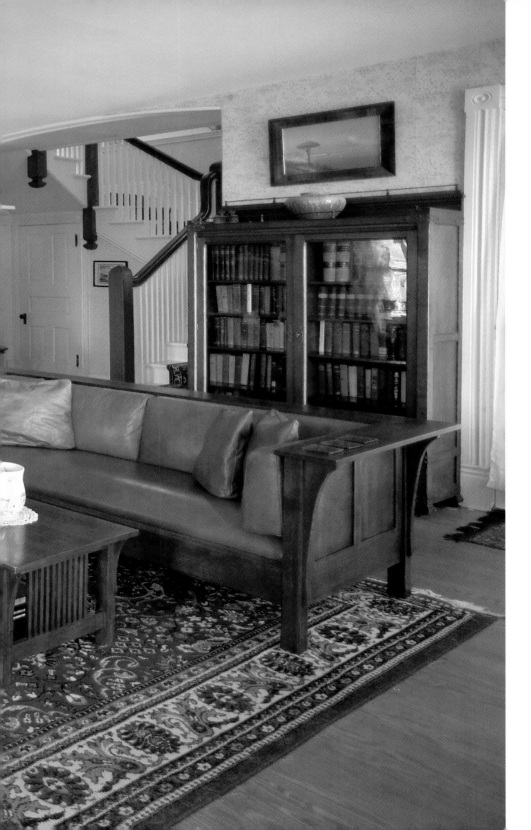

In the living room, a group of furniture consists of Stickley reissues of earlier Mission designs.

Left: *The original 1910 Gustav Stickley dining set has a china cabinet filled with the cottage dinner service, made in Hong Kong and China.*

Right: *An elaborate doorway decorated with wooden spindles heralds the dining room.*

Dashwood / Himes Island, 1903

Sited majestically on close to five wooded acres with cascading lawns and gardens, this grand Neoclassical cottage has an expansive verandah with Tuscan columns high above a sweeping expanse of Canadian waters. It is set in the shadow of the Thousand Islands Bridge.

The island takes its name from Lieutenant Colonel Charles Dashwood, the third son of an English baron, as recorded in the first commercial river charts prepared by the British Admiralty Office in London. In 1900 the island was sold to a Canadian contractor, Michael P. Davis, who constructed the 13,000 sq. ft. island manor with pump house, water tower, boathouse, bathhouse, icehouse, greenhouse, and gazebo. In that era, it was notable for electric lights and a telephone system from the main house to the boathouse. While construction began in 1900, final flourishes were added in 1903.

In 1923 the property was sold to Joseph Hendrix Himes, who had served a term in the U. S. House of Representatives, and who would become controller general of the United States. He renamed the island after himself and also named the cottage Opawaka, an Indian word for "swift waters" and a reference to the river, which runs at about six knots off the grand front entrance and dock, deep enough to accommodate large boats. Upon his death in 1960, the property was donated to the Wesley Theological Seminary in Washington; subsequently, a board member of the seminary purchased the property. In 1987 it was purchased by the current owner, who spotted it when cruising the river.

Today the river verandah with classical balustrade is filled with original wicker and hung with myriad baskets of geraniums. Inside, off the central entrance hall, both living and dining rooms bear fireplaces with classical columns. The billiards room has a massive pool table, reportedly once owned by Diamond Jim Brady. The kitchen has been renovated, with moldings brought in to replicate those in the formal front rooms, adapting former staff space to changing times. Off the kitchen, the butler's pantry houses some old English china. There are fourteen bedrooms and ten bathrooms upstairs; the family bedrooms are filled with vestiges of the past, from Royal Doulton china to old lanterns, and have expansive views of the river and grounds. To the rear of the house is the servants' wing. In the basement, a chapel is another remnant of the past. Nearby is the contemporary wine room.

Stone pathways weave around the grounds, past the restored water tower, the icehouse, and an early 1900s bell tower. A clearing in groves of old oak and tall pine offers space for a badminton court or a game of horseshoes. The current owner has been replanting evergreens to keep a sense of the pristine wild on the island.

Off Dashwood Island, across luminous waters, is tiny Flag Island, which bears a flagpole and one tree. The bridge to the island was recently restored.

A winterized boathouse with living quarters is used during the spring and fall. It is home to the boat *My Own*—a 36' sedan runabout with enclosed cabin that was built in 1925 by the Hutchinson Boat Works of Alexandria Bay for the wife of Congressman Himes. It was acquired by the current owner, restored, and returned to its original domicile.

Tuscan columns line the porch that overlooks an expanse of Canadian waters; the space is used for dining in warm weather.

Left: *In the living room, the original piano is set into an alcove flanking the Neoclassical, columned fireplace.*

Right: *Above the dining room mantel, the painting of Constantinople by artist Carl Calusd is part of a collection of his work throughout the house.*

The billiard room. Reportedly, the magnificent table seen here was once owned by Diamond Jim Brady.

*The gazebo, built of river rock, is situated
on the southwestern point of the island.
Originally flanked by terraces of flowers,
it is now surrounded by pine trees.*

Boldt Yacht House, 1903

Such was hotelier George Boldt's passion for yachting that his fantastical yacht house continued to serve as a seat of his island estates long after the construction of his ill-fated castle was stopped. Built on Wellesley Island in 1903, it was designed by castle architects George W. and William D. Hewitt of Philadelphia. The National Register of Historic Places described the landmark as "an eclectic tour de force unsurpassed in the estate architecture of the St. Lawrence Region." Noting that the yacht house was "built to reflect the towers, spires and steep-pitched gables of Boldt's 'Castle' mansion across the channel," the report added, "the yacht house is a monumental example of the 'Shingle Style' architecture characteristic of fashionable resort and recreation areas during the early twentieth century."

It was designed with three prefabricated yacht bays, with an additional fourth bay created to accommodate the houseboat *La Duchesse*. A cupola created the draft to harness the exhaust from both steam and gasoline engines, and seven pairs of screw jacks provided the mechanism for raising the yachts for service. Adjoining the yacht bays, the circular tower beckoned with reception rooms. According to the National Register report, they were "characterized by decorative oak ceilings, moldings and wainscoting, ornate carved stair balusters and newel posts, and fireplaces of cut and fitted stone." Also housed within the yacht house are caretaker's quarters—a residence for the superintendent of the fleet or of the Boldt estates.

The architects selected materials indigenous to the river for the yacht house. "The conscious use of native construction materials such as granite, pine, and cedar shingles to blend the massive yacht house with its rustic island surroundings is a further reflection of the Hewitts' sensitivity to contemporary architectural trends," noted the National Register report.

Built originally of prefabricated bays, the yacht house shelters PDQ (Pretty Damn Quick).
both a Gold Cup race boat and a Boldt family legacy.

*The living quarters for the superintendent
of the fleet included a reception room with
decorative oak ceiling and wainscoting.*

Boldt Castle, 1904

It was to be the culmination of the American dream, an island castle for his wife Louise, just as George Boldt was achieving prominence as the leading hotelier in America. Boldt, an ambitious Prussian immigrant, had risen from assistant steward at the venerable Philadelphia Club—where he had met his wife, daughter of the chief steward—to manager and president of the Waldorf-Astoria in New York City and owner of the Bellevue-Stratford in Philadelphia.

In the 1890s, he commissioned the Philadelphia society architects G. W. and W. D. Hewitt to design a 120-room residence on Hart Island. In honor of his wife, whose birthday fell on Valentine's Day, he changed the island shape and name to Heart. "He would build his lovely Louise a castle like the castles on the Rhine he'd seen in Germany as a child," recalls his granddaughter Clover Boldt Baird in the small book *The Love Story of Boldt Castle*.

With plans finalized in 1900, an army of three hundred workmen assembled on the island to begin constructing the castle from granite taken from an Oak Island quarry, also owned by Boldt. Even the plans for the greenhouses included a castellated tower and palm house. Porches rimmed the castle. Inside, principal first-floor rooms included the reception room, billiards room, library, central hall with grand staircase, as well as the ballroom, dining room, kitchen with servants' dining room, and Mr. Boldt's office. In the basement was a small swimming pool. Outbuildings also were designed as castles. The power house utilized coal brought by barge to produce steam for a generator to make electricity for the castle. The Alster Tower, designed for recreation, was replete with a small theatrical stage, a café, and a bowling alley.

Four years and two million dollars after construction had begun, as the castle neared completion, tragedy struck. A telegram sent to the superintendent of construction simply stated, "Stop the work. Mrs. Boldt is dead." She was thirty-two-years old. Although Boldt returned to the Thousand Islands, to his fifty-two-room Wellesley House on Wellesley Island, he never returned to Heart Island. The unfinished castle entered an era of decline. In 1925, the Boldt estate with castle and two thousand five hundred acres on the river was purchased by E. J. Noble, who had founded the Life Savers Candy Company and later owned the American Broadcasting Company (ABC).

Today a symbol of love lost and a dashed dream, Boldt Castle commands a steady stream of visitors by boat, eager to explore the legacy. The unfinished castle has enjoyed a renaissance in recent years, since its acquisition in 1977 by the Thousand Islands Bridge Authority. The Boldt family crest is prominently displayed: a hart (or deer) is placed atop a heart inscribed with the letter B. In a long-term plan for rehabilitation, most of the principal rooms have been reconstructed, with marble flooring throughout and a grand central staircase with stained-glass dome. An elevator has been installed in a once empty cage. A shuttle launch connects Heart Island with the Yacht House, located nearby on Wellesley Island, another vestige of George Boldt's dream of an island empire.

Columns of granite—the same stone used in the castle's construction—flank the reconstructed porch, which has a beaded fir ceiling.

Left: *The power house was equipped with a generator, providing electricity to the island.*

Right: *Flanked by ferns, the reception room has its original plasterwork replicated.*

Left: *Once a skeletal structure in the unfinished castle, the staircase has been reconstructed in oak and marble.*

Right: *The ballroom, featuring an ornate plasterwork ceiling with an oval inlay, overlooks the East Lawn and dovecote.*

The new stained-glass dome—housed in framework original to the castle and decorated with hearts—is located above the grand staircase.

La Duchesse, 1903

At the dawn of summer, *La Duchesse*—a 106' houseboat launched in 1903 and the grand dame of the St. Lawrence River—reigned from her new moorings at the Antique Boat Museum. "She's looking good, isn't she?" asked Edward "Teddy" McNally, now chairman of the museum board, gazing at the stately houseboat where he spent childhood summers. His late father, Andrew McNally—former chairman of Rand McNally, the map company founded by the latter's great-grandfather and namesake—had reclaimed the boat from the river in 1943 and had it restored.

That day, McNally arrived at the Clayton, New York, museum at the helm of the *Kon-Tiki*, a sleek 1932 Gar Wood runabout of burnished mahogany named after the Rand McNally best seller. *Kon-Tiki* bears the McNally private signal flag on the bow, a globe set on a blue background. "It's North and South America, with a sense of other continents on either side," he said. At the gala opening of *La Duchesse*, the four flags traditionally raised flew once again: the U.S. flag, the McNally private signal, the New York State flag, and the Ontario provincial flag.

Wooden boats with panache are the genesis of legends on the upper St. Lawrence River. During the Gilded Age, as captains of industry built grand island compounds, they amassed great fleets of yachts, race boats and runabouts, skiffs and canoes, for river outings. Many are preserved at the museum today. In 1986, McNally bequeathed *La Duchesse* to the museum, with a lifetime tenancy, thus sparking the growth of the pleasure boating museum. The houseboat was designed by the New York firm of Tams, LeMoine and Crane, who would help define the quintessential yacht of America in that era.

La Duchesse was built for George Boldt, then manager of the Waldorf-Astoria in New York City. "Imagine a smallish Gilded Age mansion on a raft," said John Summers, then chief curator at the Antique Boat Museum, speaking to Preservation Online. Aboard *La Duchesse*, a paneled formal salon with marble fireplace has gold-leaf stenciling on a canvas ceiling, a coffered stained-glass window, and a Steinway piano decorated with a painting of Mozart with a nymph. An expansive open deck is furnished with wicker. Downstairs, the formal dining room has a brass fireplace decorated with shells, starfish, and Admiralty dolphins—once pointed out by the late McNally as his "favorite thing." There are seven staterooms, with Pullman shades, and galley and crew quarters.

In the early 1940s, *La Duchesse* was a damsel in distress, partially sunken in the waters of the Boldt Castle Yacht House. Boldt's dreams for an island castle had been dashed when his wife died suddenly; later, his estate, with boats, was acquired by Edward J. Noble, founder of the Life Savers Candy Company and owner of the American Broadcasting Company (ABC). Mr. McNally arranged with his friend Noble to remove her from the yacht house, and finalized the sale of *La Duchesse* for $100.

Until May 2005, the restored *La Duchesse* had been berthed off the twenty-eight-acre family island compound, bedecked each summer with flowers grown by McNally in his gardens. Then a new era began as the houseboat was towed ten miles upriver to the museum, escorted by McNally and his daughter, Heather, in the *Kon-Tiki*. "She was chugging along," said McNally, estimating the houseboat speed at about seven knots. Prior to the bittersweet voyage, he said, "Dad had a very strong sense of history, and the history of the houseboat is very tied to the river. This is hopefully a means of preserving it forever."

The upper deck of the 106-foot houseboat traditionally has been bedecked with flowers.

Left: *A study is part of the master bedroom suite.*

Right: *The brass fireplace in the dining room is decorated with shells, starfish, and Admiralty dolphins.*

A stained-glass skylight is located
in the formal, paneled salon above
the Steinway piano.

Bostwick Island, 1905

Tucked into the woods, this Bungalow Style cottage is the centerpiece of a twelve-acre compound on Canadian waters. Two flags, U.S. and Canadian, dominate the skyline. Low to the ground, with a hipped roof and dormers, the bungalow was built in 1905. It subsequently was acquired in the Depression era as a guest cottage for neighboring Oakden Island. The father of the current owner purchased it half a century ago, and today cottage life beckons to four generations.

An Arts & Crafts inscription, partially attributed to William Shakespeare, decorates the large covered front porch and welcomes guests: "Beseech Ye sirs, be merry, Ye have cause, So have we all of joy. The pipe of peace does incense burn for valued guest return." The porch faces north and west for striking sunsets. Grandchildren play cards by candlelight.

The pine-floored boathouse is a locus of activity. With rebuilt stone cribs reinforced by steel, the boathouse is home to a gleaming replica of a 1938 Gar Wood racing boat, *Limit Up*, which takes its name from trading talk on the futures exchange. From the boathouse, walkways lined with impatiens weave up to the cottage and throughout the lushly landscaped grounds, with vistas and island vignettes oriented toward the luminous river.

A large garden room, shadowed by great oak and hemlock trees, was created by bringing in barge-loads of soil. A nature trail winds through the woods of the eighty-six-acre island; wildlife sighted includes deer, fox, raccoon, and even muskrat. Elsewhere on the compound, a stone lookout bench is sited high above the river, a prime spot for sunset watching. Creature comforts include a hot tub, perched on a rocky ledge, and a sauna, nestled into the woods.

Much has changed with island life. Gone are the days when a mail boat delivered letters to a box at the end of the dock. The technological revolution has made it possible for the owner to maintain business communications when on the island. And, in the event of a power outage, there is a backup generator. Yet, as the season becomes more extended, some things remain constant—the cottage is warmed in early spring and late fall by the fireplace of native island rock.

Limit Up, *a replica of a 1938 Gar Wood racing boat, takes its name from trading talk on the futures exchange.*

An expansive porch provides open views to the water.

Left: *The deep eaves and exposed rafters of the bedroom are characteristic of the bungalow style.*

Right: *The bedroom is paneled in pine.*

Dark Island, 1905

This historic structure was built as a hunting lodge. Frederick Bourne, who commissioned it, was the son of a minister who had risen to become president of The Singer Manufacturing Company and commodore of the New York Yacht Club. A dramatic addition to the Chippewa Bay skyline, the castle was finished in 1905 after three years of construction. *The New York Times* lauded it as a "Castle of Mysteries," stating that "in a structure resembling an Old World Castle he has incorporated some of the architectural mysteries that always appeal to one as being an inherent part of every castle, dungeon-deep passages, mysterious doorways in sliding panels, and secret peepholes."

The twenty-eight-room castle, designed by architect Ernest Flagg, was sited on almost seven rugged island acres and was called The Towers because of two prominent towers. Flagg had been the architect of Bourne's palatial Long Island estate, Indian Neck Hall, and would go on in 1908 to design the acclaimed Singer Building, then the tallest building in the world. In the Thousand Islands, The Towers was built of stone quarried on Oak Island. It was inspired by a fictional castle—a royal hunting lodge from Sir Walter Scott's novel *Woodstock*. It required a staff of forty to maintain the castle and outbuildings that included two boathouses designed for yachts. The north boathouse featured an underground passage to the castle.

Bourne had requested that the grounds be left in their rugged beauty with the exception of a formal walled garden. Outside amenities included a tall clock tower with chimes, high above the river, and grass tennis courts with a pergola for viewing the matches. Indoors, amenities included a six hundred-bottle wine cellar. After Bourne's death, in 1919 daughters Marjorie Bourne and May Strassburger acquired Dark Island from their siblings for $389,000; Marjorie Bourne made several additions, including a squash court and a sports therapy room. She also enclosed the loggia room.

The entrance hall to the castle is a vaulted, cavernous space. Stone steps lead up to the paneled library, which has a secret panel next to the fireplace. Another staircase provides access to the main floor, with principal rooms led by the trophy room, or drawing room; there, Pullman-style booths line the walls and were originally intended for gaming. In the formal dining room with marble fireplace, the hand-carved oak table has griffin legs and features the original call button underneath it. Off the loggia is a sunroom filled with wicker furniture. Upstairs, beyond the family and guest suites, the fourth floor is dominated by a large dormitory room.

When Marjorie Bourne Thayer died in 1962, she had deeded Dark Island to the La Salle Christian Brothers, who sold it to Dr. Harold Martin, a minister who invited the public to Sunday chapel services at the castle during the summer months. In 2002 he sold the castle to an investment group who opened it for public tours.

A crenelated wall lines the walk leading to the medieval-inspired castle.

This page: *The restored rose garden is planted with English roses and heirloom flowers.*

Next page:

Top: In the hunting lodge, the trophy room served as the drawing room.

Bottom—left and right: *The dining room*

Bluff Island, 1910

With its dramatic siting and vivid color, this Colonial Revival cottage is a beacon on the American channel. The granite of the high foundation wall came from neighboring Picton Island. The Neoclassical pediment and dormers, reflecting the local taste for a complexity of roofline, are framed by the island panorama of woods and sky.

Bluff Island is rife with the early history of the river. The Indians of the Confederation of Five Nations are said to have met on the bluff of the island, whether using it as a campsite or a vantage point for long views up and down the river. The soil of the island has a high clay content, and chards of the pottery made by the Indians have been found in contemporary times. In 1760 the St. Lawrence was the site of the Battle of the Thousand Islands in the French and Indian War, resulting in a British-Iroquois victory. A button believed to be from the uniform of a French soldier is a memento found and prized by the owner of this cottage.

The cottage, acquired by the current owner in 1978, is built of South Carolina pine and has oak floors. It has survived three fires. The large porch, partially enclosed, is a favorite place to watch the daily parade of boats. Traditions here include watching the Fourth of July fireworks emanating from Clayton, New York. Other gatherings for "river rats"—an honorary title for those seasoned denizens of the river who are privy to its secrets and its shoals—have included supper parties with dancing.

Inside the cottage, a large stone hearth dominates the living room. In the dining room, the walls are hung with antique maps of the county, and the oak furniture is original to the cottage. Upstairs, there are seven bedrooms, all with gleaming wood walls and views of the ever-changing river.

Outside, a former caretaker's log cabin is a relic of days gone by, secluded behind the cottage and tucked into the woods. The owners enjoy communing with nature and have created a preserve from the natural rock and pool formations, which abut a small sand beach. The placid pools, adorned with floating water lilies, are stocked with koi. Domestic ducks from California have been introduced to the environment. The bird life is abundant and includes mourning doves, finches, sparrows, and ravens. "We take a walk every morning and listen to the bird life," says the owner. "It's music." A shuffleboard court was discovered when gardening; the grounds also have a vegetable garden and a strawberry patch, a reflection of the agrarian roots of the region.

Left: *A bright, open porch allows for casual contemplation of the waterway.*
Page 194: *In the dining room, the oak furniture is original to the cottage, and antique maps line the walls.*
Page 195: *All of the bedrooms in the pine-paneled cottage have river views.*

Above: *Brought from California and raised by the owner, ducks take to a pool in a nature preserve created on the island.*

Left: *A screened sun porch allows for quiet contemplation of the water.*

Napoleon's Hat, Hay Island, 1913

This enigmatic cottage, with its exotic motifs, takes its name from the curving roofline and its resemblance to the Emperor Napoleon's hat. Inside, the owners have indulged their penchant for Napoleon memorabilia. With the look of a diminutive dollhouse, it enchanted the illustrator John Striebel, who featured it in his syndicated *Dixie Dugan* cartoon strip. "Isn't it darling?" remarked a character in the cartoon, as voyagers by boat neared Napoleon's Hat. It was the first cottage to be built on Hay Island in Canadian waters. The current guest cottage, built in 1897, was the fishing house. The cottage overlooks the forty-acre shoal, a famed fishing ground.

The cottage was built by business partners Walter Staebler and Godfrey Baker, whose company bearing their names is now the Graphic Controls Corporation. It is a mystery to the current owners how such exotic architecture came into being on this secluded island. With no right angles, the cottage is anchored by three circular rooms with spade-shaped windows. The circular foyer, dining room, and kitchen, all open onto the living room and its Napoleon displays.

The nucleus of the Napoleon memorabilia was acquired at a Kingston, Ontario, auction and ranges from paintings to tea sets with battle scenes to toy soldiers. Today house guests are likely to arrive bearing Napoleon mementos. And visitors are numerous. In the boathouse, the back wall is lined with Polaroid snapshots of all guests that have visited; they range from a Crown Prince of Japan, a roving cultural ambassador, to the actress Helen Hayes. "It's our rogue's gallery—a history of friends and family," says the owner.

In keeping with the French theme, the owners purchased fabrics at country markets in France and brought home suitcases of materials in the color scheme of yellow, blue, and white. It complements an inherited collection of Wedgwood, also displayed in the living room.

Outside, the grounds beckon for exploration, with vegetable and herb gardens and a tiny tree house.

An exotic motif, whose origin is an enigma, surrounds the entrance door and is found throughout the cottage.

Left: *Fabrics for drapery were found in French country markets.*

Right: *Through the kitchen window, the cottage overlooks the 40-acre shoal, a famed fishing ground.*

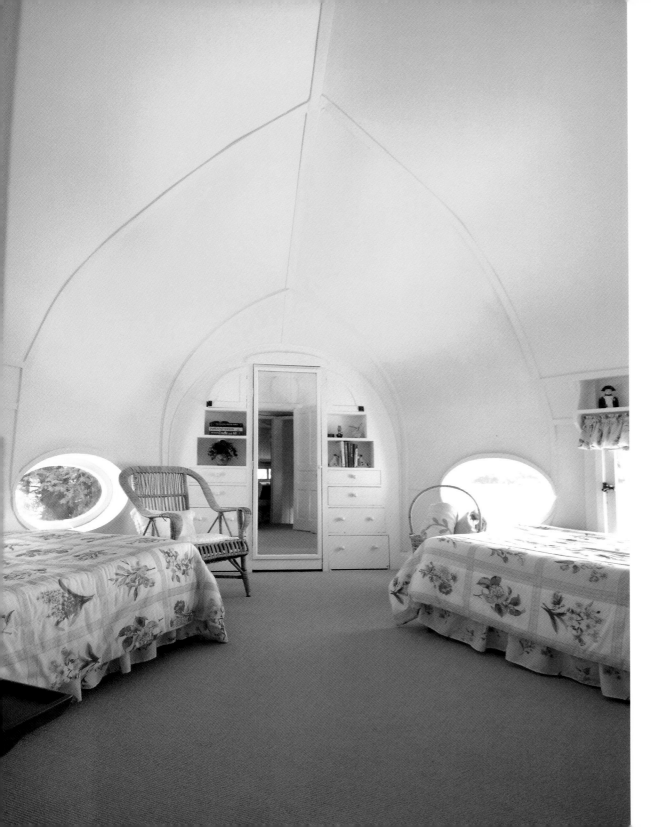

Left: *From a yellow-painted bedroom, low, elliptical windows overlook the river and wooded island.*

Right: *In the master bedroom, fabric drapes the ceiling and lines the walls.*

*The foyer is circular, as are
the dining room and kitchen.*

Fox Run, 1990

A Palladian-inspired villa, Fox Run is surrounded by eleven garden rooms carved into the landscape of some thirty-two acres, the former backside of a farm. With a Greek sundial painted onto the stucco facade that is augmented by tall pilasters, the villa is sited dramatically high on a stone cliff seventy-five feet above the St. Lawrence River. There are mesmerizing views of the quiet, rippling waters.

Classical columns are the leitmotif, both inside and out. They frame the living room, filled with antiques both French and exotic. The columns also grace the garden rooms, where the original landscape includes a natural stream and an old stone quarry space discovered during excavations. A visitor first glimpses a "little Stonehenge," created from large slabs of natural river rock, which hints at the gardens that unfold beyond it. Heralding the gardens also is a forest of natural arborvitae with its air of the primeval; the trees have been conserved.

The villa entranceways are accessed by rock terraces; thyme grows between the cracks. The oldest part of the structure, a stone cottage cube, was created in 1990 as a vacation house for Mary and Morse Dial; it was augmented by a fern and birch garden. Subsequently, the villa addition was created with the assistance of Grater Architects from Clayton, New York. One can see the former owners' passion for objets d'art in the skylighted living room. An old iron grate serves as the dining room table; the silk covers of eighteenth-century French chairs are stenciled with a fern pattern. Minerva Chapman—an aunt of the former owner who lived in Paris at the turn-of-the-twentieth century—painted the French landscapes that hang from the walls. The living room opens to the orangerie, sited high above the water, with an enamel stove from Italy.

There is a constant sense of discovery in the gardens. Freestanding columns define The Oracle, a temple-like structure named by the artist Marc Leuthold and sited alongside the stream, with a waterfall that flows to the river. In the forest, a gazebo beckons, covered with leafy green hops. Flat rocks have been transformed into furniture. In the meditation garden, framed by Victorian white birches and five locust trees, there is a natural rock floor; a stone throne chair awaits. A freestanding structure overlooking the quarry garden, the garden house was inspired by old Palladian windows found in a Connecticut antique shop. It has a daybed and an old marble sink supported by birch tree columns. Ferns are painted on the furniture and on the floor. Also on the grounds is the Hemlock House, an A-frame with loft, used as a guest cottage and tucked into a hemlock forest. And, far removed from the complex is an artist's one-room cabin, replete with a sweeping rock terrace high above the river; a sandstone chaise longue beckons for contemplating the muse.

A garden house, inspired by old Palladian windows found in an antiques shop,
overlooks a cavernous garden room created in a former stone quarry.

Left: *A garden folly, the Oracle is composed of classical columns and is sited next to a natural stream and waterfall.*

Right: *The loggia, with panoramic views, is situated a dramatic seventy-five feet above the St. Lawrence River.*

A passion for things French, from paintings to furniture, mingles with the exotic in the living/dining room of the villa. Columns grace the perimeter of the room.

215

Bluff Island, 1990

T his guest cottage, sited on a promontory on the river, was designed as a paean to shelter and nature. The owner, whose family spans five generations on the river, grew up on neighboring Murray Island and had picnicked on Bluff Island as a child, subsequently purchasing a cottage there. In 1990 it was decided to build the guest cottage over a gully, a major island undertaking. "It was designed to be very small and very private, to blend into the woods," says the owner, who has hosted guests such as Hillary and Bill Clinton there.

Local builder Steve Taylor, who previously had brought his expertise to the remodeling of the main house, designed the pavilion-like guest cottage with generous overhangs. With views to the north and west, for magnificent sunsets, the house is supported by concrete piers and has cantilevered decks. All rooms open to the outdoors, with exterior hallways accessing the decks.

Inside, the main living area is dominated by a massive granite fireplace; a side staircase leads up to the sleeping loft above the kitchen and dining area. The kitchen is set under the eaves. "The kitchen was to be part of the living pattern of the house," says Taylor. In another wing of the L-shaped plan, parallel to the river, are the master bedroom, the guest bedroom, two bathrooms, and an outdoor shower. "It's livable, comfortable—a simple cabin," says the owner.
With a nod to nostalgia, building materials evoke the turn-of-the-century cottages along the river. "We wanted to use local materials in a new way," said Taylor. "Modern living calls for relaxed open living plans, where the older plans were more formal. The finish materials of local granite, cedar, fir, and pine are the shared language of both old and new."

A great granite fireplace dominates the main living area.

Left: *The open living
plan is a nod to
contemporary design
and departs from the
traditional, more
formal plans of the
early cottages.*

Right:

Top: *The sleeping
alcove is located
above the kitchen
and dining area.*

Bottom: *The master
bedroom opens onto an
exterior hallway that is
accessible to the deck.*

"From this view, the sunset is spectacular,"
says an owner. The telescope is used for
boat and bird watching; subjects of
the latter include loons, ducks, geese,
ospreys, and great blue herons.